D1406196

A Book of Cradle Songs

A Book of Cradle Songs

Selected and Arranged by MARJORIE M. WYCKOFF
Illustrated by MASHA

Originally Designed and Produced by Artists and Writers Guild, Inc.
And Distributed by GROSSET & DUNLAP, *New York*

This edition published by
THE NEUMANN PRESS

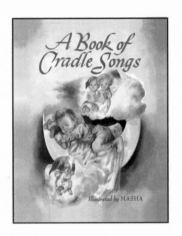

A BOOK OF CRADLE SONGS

© 2003 THE NEUMANN PRESS
© 2003 MASTERPIECE CLASSICS

ISBN: 1-930873-91-3

PRINTED, BOUND AND PUBLISHED IN THE UNITED STATES OF AMERICA
THE NEUMANN PRESS, LONG PRAIRIE, MINNESOTA

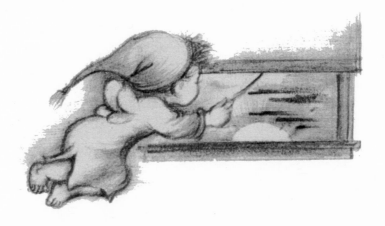

THE SANDMAN COMES

Old German Melody

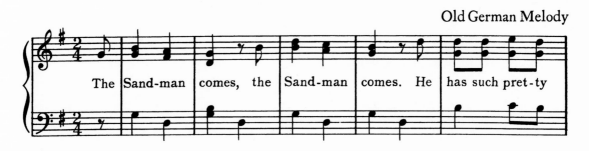

The Sand-man comes, the Sand-man comes. He has such pret-ty

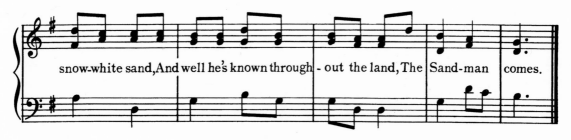

snow-white sand, And well he's known through - out the land, The Sand-man comes.

6

CRADLE SONG

From the German   Johannes Brahms

Lul - la - by   and good   night;   with   ros - es be -

dight,   With   lil - ies be - decked   is   ba - by's wee

bed;   Lay thee   down   now and   rest,   May thy   slum - ber be

8

blest; Lay thee down now and rest, May thy slum-ber be blest.

Lullaby and good night, thy mother's delight.
Bright angels around my darling shall stand;
They will guard thee from harms;
Thou shalt wake in my arms;
They will guard thee from harms,
Thou shalt wake in my arms.

ROCK-A-BYE BABY

Traditional

Rock-a-bye, ba - by on the tree top, When the wind blows the cra - dle will rock, When the bough breaks the cra - dle will fall. Down will come ba - by, cra - dle, and all.

10

CRADLE HYMN

J. J. Rousseau

Isaac Watts

Hush, my babe, lie still and slum - ber; Ho - ly an - gels guard thy bed, Heav'n - ly bless - ings with - out num - ber, Gent - ly fall - ing on thy head. How much bet - ter thou'rt at - ten - ded Than the Son of God could be, When from Heav - en He de - scend - ed, And be - came a child like thee.

Soft and easy is thy cradle;
Coarse and hard thy Savior lay,
When His birthplace was a stable,
And His softest bed was hay.
Oh, to tell the wondrous story,
How His foes abused their King;
How they killed the Lord of Glory,
Makes me angry while I sing.

Hush, my child, I did not chide thee,
Though my song may seem so hard.
'Tis thy mother sits beside thee,
And her arms shall be thy guard.
May'st thou learn to know and fear Him,
Love and serve Him all thy days;
Then to dwell forever near Him,
Tell His love and sing His praise.

SWEET AND LOW

Alfred Tennyson

Sir Joseph Barnby

Sweet and low, sweet and low, Wind of the west - ern sea:

Low, low, breathe and blow, Wind of the west - ern sea;

15

O - ver the roll - ing wa - ters go, Come from the dy - ing

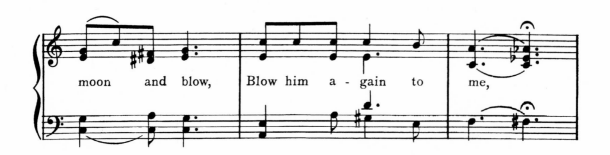

moon and blow, Blow him a - gain to me,

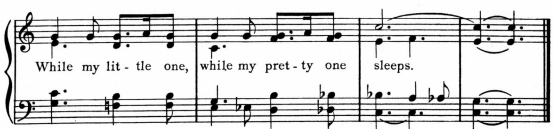

While my lit - tle one, while my pret - ty one sleeps.

Sleep and rest, sleep and rest,
Father will come to thee soon;
Rest, rest, on mother's breast,
Father will come to thee soon;

Father will come to his babe
   in the nest.
Silver sails all out of the west,
Under the silver moon;

Sleep, my little one,
Sleep, my pretty one, sleep.

BYE BABY BUNTING

Traditional

Bye, ba - by bunt - ing, Dad-dy's gone a - hunt - ing, To get a lit - tle rab - bit skin, To wrap his ba - by bunt - ing in.

SCHUBERT'S CRADLE SONG

Poet unkown

Franz Schubert

Slumber, slumber, little faded flower.
Still doth mother's love around thee glow;
Stronger is it than earthly power,
Guarding thee where'er thy spirit go.

SLEEP, SLEEP, MY DARLING

From the French

French lullaby

Slowly

Sleep, sleep, my dar-ling, sleep peace-ful - ly; Moth-er is watch-ing,

pray-ing for thee. May ho-ly an-gels on wings of light, Bring to my

ba - by, dreams fair and bright. Do-do, my dar-ling, peace-ful-ly sleep.

Sleep, sleep, my darling, sleep peacefully;
Thy heav'nly Father careth for thee;
In thy soft cradle peacefully sleep;
While thou dost slumber, watch He will keep.
Dodo, my darling, peacefully sleep.

RUSSIAN LULLABY

Circassian Melody

Sleep, ah sleep, my dar-ling ba-by, Su su lul-la-by;

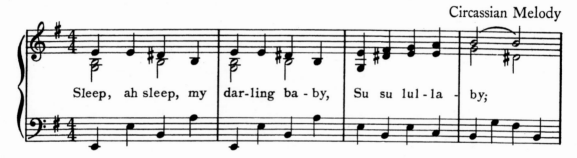

See, the moon is watch-ing o'er thee, Peace-ful-ly on high.

Thou shalt hear a wondrous story;
Close each wakeful eye;
And a song as well I'll sing thee,
Su, su, lullaby.

ALL THROUGH THE NIGHT

Old Welsh Air

Sleep, my child, and peace at-tend thee, All through the night;

Guard-ian an-gels God will lend thee, All through the night;

Soft the drow-sy hours are creep-ing, Hill and vale in slum-ber steep-ing,

I my lov-ing vig-il keep-ing, All through the night.

26

While the moon her watch is keeping,
All through the night;
While the weary world is sleeping,
All through the night;

O'er thy spirit gently stealing,
Visions of delight revealing,
Breathes a pure and holy feeling,
All through the night.

INDIAN LULLABY

Charles Myall

Marjorie M. Wyckoff

Rock-a-bye, hush-a-by, lit-tle pap-poose, The stars come

in-to the sky, The whip-poor-will's cry-ing, The day-light is dy-ing, The

riv-er runs mur-mur-ing by.

The breezes are pining, the moonbeams
are shining
All over the prairie wide.
Then hush-a-bye, rock-a-bye, little
papoose,
You sail on the river of dreams;
Dear Manitou loves you, and watches
above you
Till time when the morning light gleams.

SLEEP, BABY, SLEEP

From the German

Sleep, ba-by, sleep! Thy
fa-ther tends the sheep; Thy
moth - er shakes the
dream-land tree, And
softly, slower
down come love - ly

dreams to thee. Sleep, ba-by, sleep! Sleep, ba-by, sleep!

Sleep, baby, sleep!
The large stars are the sheep;
The little ones, the lambs, I guess,
The gentle moon, the shepherdess.
Sleep, baby, sleep!
Sleep, baby, sleep!

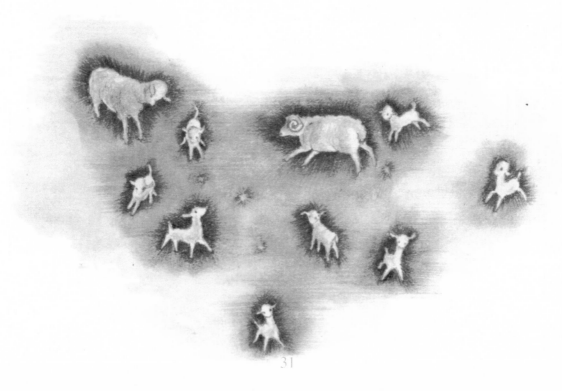

SCOTCH LULLABY

Sir Walter Scott

T. Whittaker

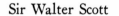

Oh, hush thee, my ba-by, Thy sire was a knight, Thy moth-er a la-dy, Both

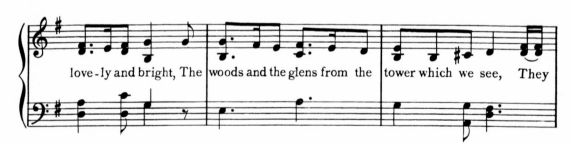

love-ly and bright, The woods and the glens from the tower which we see, They

all are be-long-ing, dear ba-by, to thee. Oh, — hush thee, my ba-by, Thy

sire was a knight, Oh, hush thee, my ba-by, So — bon-nie, so — bright.

Oh, fear not the bugle,
Though loudly it blows.
It calls but the wardens
That guard thy repose;

Their bows would be bended,
Their blades would be red,
Ere the step of the foeman
Draws near to thy bed.

NOW THE DAY IS OVER

S. Baring Gould

Sir Joseph Barnby

Now the day is o - ver; Night is draw - ing nigh;

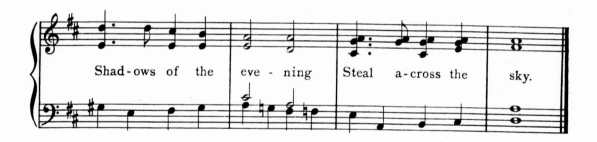

Shad - ows of the eve - ning Steal a - cross the sky.

Now the darkness gathers;
Stars begin to peep;
Birds and beasts and flowers
Soon will be asleep.

MY BED IS LIKE A LITTLE BOAT

Robert Louis Stevenson

Marjorie M. Wyckoff

Jauntily, but not fast

My bed is like a lit-tle boat, Nurse helps me in when I em-bark. She

girds me on my sail-or's coat, And starts me in the dark.

At night, I go on board and say
Good night to all my friends on shore;
I shut my eyes and sail away
And see and hear no more.

And sometimes things to bed I take,
As prudent sailors have to do;
Perhaps a slice of wedding-cake,
Perhaps a toy or two.

All night across the dark we steer;
But when the day returns at last,
Safe in my room, beside the pier,
I find my vessel fast.